TABLE OF C

1 - SETTINGS AND SAFETY — 5
2 - ESSENTIAL TOOLS AND ACCESSORIES — 6
3 - WHY CROCKPOT? BENEFITS UNVEILED — 7
4 - THE SCIENCE OF SLOW COOKING — 8
5 - COMMON MISTAKES AND HOW TO AVOID THEM — 9
6 - GLOSSARY OF CROCKPOT TERMS — 10

CHICKEN

- CHICKEN AND VEGGIE STEW — 11
- CHICKEN WITH ROSEMARY AND ROOT VEGETABLES — 12
- TARRAGON LEMON CHICKEN — 13
- CHICKEN RATATOUILLE — 14
- HERBED CHICKEN AND LENTIL SOUP — 15
- TOMATO BASIL CHICKEN — 16
- CURRIED CHICKEN AND CAULIFLOWER — 17

TURKEY

- MOROCCAN TURKEY AND CHICKPEA STEW — 18
- MAPLE-DIJON GLAZED TURKEY — 19
- TURKEY AND SWEET POTATO HASH — 20
- TURKEY BOLOGNESE WITH ZUCCHINI NOODLES — 21
- ASIAN-INSPIRED TURKEY LETTUCE WRAPS — 22
- TURKEY AND KALE CHILI — 23
- CRANBERRY GLAZED TURKEY BREAST — 24

PORK

- PORK AND BROCCOLI CASSEROLE — 25
- BALSAMIC GLAZED PORK TENDERLOIN — 26
- TUSCAN PORK AND BEAN SOUP — 27
- PORK AND CABBAGE ROLL-UPS — 28
- ROSEMARY ORANGE PORK ROAST — 29
- MAPLE-DIJON PORK CHOPS — 30
- PORK WITH HERBED QUINOA — 31

BEEF

- GARLIC-THYME BEEF STEW — 32
- ZESTY LEMON BEEF SKEWERS — 33
- BEEF AND SPINACH CASSEROLE — 34
- LEMON-PEPPER BEEF STEAKS — 35
- BEEF, CABBAGE, AND CARROT SOUP — 36
- BEEF AND BUTTERNUT SQUASH STEW — 37
- BEEF AND VEGETABLE RATATOUILLE — 38

TABLE OF CONTENTS

LAMB

TUSCAN LAMB AND ARTICHOKE STEW	39
LAMB AND ASPARAGUS STIR FRY	40
LAMB WITH CILANTRO AND LIME	41
LAMB AND EGGPLANT RAGOUT	42
LAMB WITH ROASTED RED PEPPER SAUCE	43
GREEK-INSPIRED LAMB AND OLIVE STEW	44
LAMB AND LENTIL STEW	45

FISH AND SEAFOOD

COD WITH LEMON AND DILL SAUCE	46
SHRIMP AND VEGETABLE CURRY	47
MISO-GLAZED TILAPIA	48
SEAFOOD PAELLA WITH SAFFRON	49
CLAM AND CORN CHOWDER	50
HERBED HALIBUT AND GREEN BEANS	51
SEAFOOD JAMBALAYA	52

VEGETARIAN

HEARTY VEGETABLE AND BEAN SOUP	53
EGGPLANT AND TOMATO RATATOUILLE	54
SPINACH AND FETA STUFFED PORTOBELLOS	55
CAULIFLOWER AND CHICKPEA TIKKA MASALA	56
SWEET POTATO AND BLACK BEAN CHILI	57
VEGETABLE AND LENTIL LOAF	58
STUFFED CABBAGE ROLLS WITH TOMATO SAUCE	59

SNACKS

LEMON-GARLIC MARINATED OLIVES	60
CROCK POT POPCORN WITH HERBS	61
WARM SPINACH AND ARTICHOKE DIP	62
ROASTED RED PEPPER HUMMUS	63
SESAME-GINGER SOY CUCUMBER SALAD	64
SLOW-COOKED GRANOLA WITH MIXED BERRIES	65
BALSAMIC GLAZED BRUSSELS SPROUT CHIPS	66

DESSERTS

VANILLA BEAN RICE PUDDING	67
MAPLE-GLAZED POACHED FIGS	68
CINNAMON APPLE CRISP WITH OAT TOPPING	69
MANGO AND PINEAPPLE SORBET	70
SLOW-COOKER CHOCOLATE-DIPPED STRAWBERRIES	71
GINGER AND APRICOT BAKED APPLES	72
ZUCCHINI CHOCOLATE CAKE	73
SLOW COOKER CARAMEL FLAN	74

★ A FREE BOOK FOR YOU ★

- **INTERESTED IN FOLLOWING A HEALTHY AND DELICIOUS DIET?**
- **LOVE FULL COLOR PICTURES AND DESCRIPTIVE RECIPES?**

★SCAN TO GET YOUR HEALTHY BOOK RIGHT NOW!★

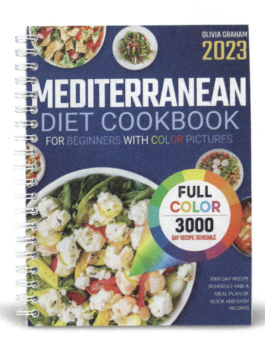 

★ALSO SCAN TO LEAVE A 5 SECOND REVIEW★

★ WHAT TO DO NOW? ★

AT THIS POINT, YOU MUST BE LOOKING FORWARD TO READING THIS BOOK AND ENJOYING THE RECIPES AND COOKING RIGHT AWAY!

BUT FIRST, DO THESE TWO THINGS! ●

STEP 1: ACCESS THE OFFER IN THE PREVIOUS PAGE AND START REAPING THE BENEFITS OF AN INCREDIBLE HEALTHY DIET!

STEP 2: LET ME KNOW HOW EXCITED YOU ARE OF HAVING THIS BOOK IN YOUR HANDS!

LEAVE A QUICK REVIEW ON AMAZON IN LESS THAN 5 SECONDS AND SHARE YOUR EXCITEMENT! ●

SCAN BELOW TO REVIEW THE BOOK QUICKLY!

DEMYSTIFYING THE CROCKPOT: SETTINGS AND SAFETY

- **Low vs. High:** Cooking on low means the food will be cooked at a lower temperature (around 200°F or 93°C) and will take longer, often 7-8 hours. High setting cooks food faster, usually in 3-4 hours, at a temperature around 300°F or 149°C.

- **Timers and Programmable Features**: Some modern crockpots come with timers that automatically switch the setting to 'warm' after a certain number of hours. This feature ensures your food doesn't overcook if you're out or forget to check.

- *Cleaning:* Wait for the crockpot to cool down before cleaning. Most removable inserts are dishwasher safe. For stubborn stains, let it soak in warm soapy water. Avoid using abrasive cleaners or pads which can damage the surface.

- *Storing:* Always ensure the crockpot is dry before storing to prevent mold. Store it in a dry place and avoid stacking heavy items on top.

- *Safety Tips:* Never start cooking in a cold crockpot; this means if it's been in a cold room, let it come to room temperature before starting. Avoid drastic temperature changes.

ESSENTIAL TOOLS AND ACCESSORIES

HOW TO INTRODUCE POTENTIAL ALLERGENS

Must-Have Tools for a Crockpot Enthusiast

Every artist needs a canvas, but the magic really happens with the brushes. Similarly, while your crockpot is the heart of the operation, these tools bring the art to life.

- **Ladles:** Ideal for soups, stews, and broths. A good ladle ensures consistent serving sizes and a no-mess transfer to bowls.

- **Tongs**: Essential for lifting or turning larger pieces of meat or vegetables without damaging them. It's all about that gentle grip!

- **Liners:** Say goodbye to strenuous cleaning. Liners protect your crockpot from getting dirty and make post-cooking clean-up a breeze.

- **Thermometer:** Ensure your meats are perfectly cooked and safe to eat. A kitchen thermometer takes the guesswork out of cooking.

- **Silicone Mitts:** Handling a hot crockpot is safer and more comfortable with silicone mitts, offering a secure grip.

WHY CROCKPOT? BENEFITS UNVEILED

- **Nutrient Retention:** Slow cooking at lower temperatures helps in preserving the vitamins and minerals in your food.

- **Less Oil Usage:** Given the extended cooking times and the sealed environment, foods release and cook in their natural juices. This reduces the need for additional oils.

- **Cost-Effective:** Slow cookers are perfect for cheaper cuts of meat. Over the slow cooking process, these tougher, often less expensive cuts become tender and flavorful, giving gourmet results on a budget.

- **Less Energy Consumption:** Despite the longer cooking times, a crockpot uses less electricity than an oven, making it energy-efficient. It's a win for your utility bill and the environment.

- **Minimal Prep:** Most crockpot recipes require minimal preparation. Toss in the ingredients, and you're done.

- **Passive Cooking:** The beauty lies in its ability to cook without constant supervision. No need to stir, check, or fret. Just set the timer, and go about your day.

THE SCIENCE OF SLOW COOKING

- *Heat Distribution:* Slow cookers use consistent and gentle heat, ensuring even cooking without the need to stir frequently.

- *Retention of Moisture:* The sealed environment prevents moisture loss, which is why stews and soups excel in a slow cooker.

- *Tenderizing Abilities:* The prolonged cooking time breaks down tough fibers, making even the most robust meats melt-in-the-mouth.

- *Longer Marination:* As the food simmers for hours, it gets ample time to absorb the essences of herbs, spices, and marinades, enhancing its taste.

- *Layering Ingredients:* Placing ingredients in a specific order can influence the final dish. Typically, hard ingredients like root vegetables go at the bottom, while delicate ones rest on top.

5 COMMON MISTAKES AND HOW TO AVOID THEM

- **Ideal Fill Level:** A crockpot should be ½ to ⅔ full. This ensures even heat distribution and optimal cooking.

- **Meat Choices:** Fattier cuts like pork shoulder or beef chuck fare better in slow cookers. They remain moist and tender, breaking down over the long cooking process.

- **Too Watery?** If your dish is too liquidy, remove the lid for the last 30 minutes to let some steam evaporate or transfer to a pot and simmer until reduced.

- **Overcooked Veggies?** Next time, layer them on top or add them halfway through. For now, blend them into a sauce or soup to mask their mushiness.

GLOSSARY OF CROCKPOT TERMS

- **Braising:** A method where the food is first seared at high temperatures, then finished in a covered pot at a lower temperature. It's perfect for turning tough cuts of meat into tender morsels. In a crockpot, this method is employed by allowing the pot's low, steady heat to slowly cook and tenderize.

- **Simmering:** Cooking liquid just below the boiling point where small bubbles form slowly. It's gentler than boiling, ensuring your ingredients don't break down too rapidly. In crockpot settings, this usually correlates to the 'low' setting.

- **Searing:** Quickly browning the surface of food at a high temperature. It's often done before slow cooking to lock in flavors and give the dish a deeper taste profile. While traditional crockpots don't sear, some modern ones come with this function, or you can sear ingredients in a pan before adding to the crockpot.

- **Stewing:** Cooking solid food ingredients that have been cut into bite-sized pieces in liquid for a long time. The crockpot is essentially a stewing champion, letting ingredients meld over hours.

- **Layering:** The strategic placement of ingredients, typically with those requiring the longest cook time (like certain meats) at the bottom. This ensures even cooking.

- **High Setting:** Cooks food faster, usually in 3-4 hours. Often used for dishes that benefit from a shorter cooking time or if you're in a bit of a hurry.

- **Low Setting:** Cooks food slower, often 6-8 hours. This is the go-to for most traditional slow cooker recipes, allowing flavors to deeply infuse.

CHICKEN AND VEGGIE STEW

320 KCAL · 2 SERVINGS · 3 HOURS

INGREDIENTS

- 2 chicken breasts, skin off (6 oz/170g each)
- 1 cheerful carrot, diced up (about 1 cup/120g)
- 2 lovely potatoes, diced (1.5 cups/230g)
- 1 welcoming onion, finely chopped (around 1/2 cup/75g)
- 2 garlic cloves, minced
- 2 cups/475 ml low-sodium chicken broth
- A tad of olive oil (1 tsp/5 ml)
- Salt 'n pepper, to your liking
- A dash of dried thyme (1/2 tsp/2.5 ml)
- Fresh parsley, chopped, as a fresh finish

NUTRITION

- **Carbs:** 35g
- **Protein:** 28g
- **Fat:** 6g
- **Fiber:** 5g
- **Omega 3:** 0.1g
- **Vitamin D:** 0.5µg
- **Calcium:** 50mg
- **Iron:** 3mg

DIRECTIONS

1. Lightly coat crockpot's bottom with olive oil.
2. In go the chicken, potatoes, carrot, onion, and garlic.
3. Drizzle the chicken broth, thyme, salt, and pepper over it all.
4. Cover up and let it simmer on low for 3 hours.
5. Before you dish out, sprinkle the parsley on top.

ALLERGENS & TIPS

Allergens: Got Chicken & Garlic in here, heads up! And sometimes, broths have hidden surprises, so always double-check.

Tips: A slice of multi-grain bread complements this stew perfectly. Also, organically sourced chicken just feels right, doesn't it? And for a twist, a bay leaf wouldn't hurt!

CHICKEN WITH ROSEMARY AND ROOT VEGETABLES

300 KCAL
2 SERVINGS
4 HOURS

INGREDIENTS

- 2 chicken thighs, skin off (5 oz/140g each)
- 1 potato, roughly chopped (about 1 cup/150g)
- 2 parsnips, sliced up (1 cup/130g)
- 1 turnip, diced (3/4 cup/115g)
- 2 sprigs of fresh rosemary
- 2 cups/475 ml low-sodium chicken broth
- A sprinkle of sea salt and fresh pepper
- 1 tsp/5 ml olive oil (just a teeny bit!)

DIRECTIONS

1. Grease the crockpot with olive oil.
2. Layer in the chicken, followed by those gorgeous root veggies.
3. Nestle in rosemary sprigs.
4. Pour the broth over, season, and let the magic happen on low for 4 hours.
5. Voilà! Perfectly tender chicken and veggies.

ALLERGENS & TIPS

Allergens: Features Chicken. Broths can be sneaky - double-check them.

Tips: Dish it up with quinoa for added protein. Organic chicken and fresh herbs? Even better! Maybe add a sprig of thyme for fun.

NUTRITION

- **Carbs: 30g**
- **Protein: 25g**
- **Fat: 5g**
- **Fiber: 6g**
- **Omega 3: 0.1g**
- **Vitamin D: 0.6µg**
- **Calcium: 48mg**
- **Iron: 2.5mg**

280 KCAL

2 SERVINGS

3.5 HOURS

TARRAGON LEMON CHICKEN

INGREDIENTS

- 2 boneless chicken breasts (about 6 oz/170g each)
- Juice of 1 lemon (about 2 tbsp/30ml)
- 1 tsp/5ml olive oil
- 2 garlic cloves, minced
- 1 tsp/5 ml dried tarragon (or 1 tbsp fresh if you have it)
- Salt and pepper to taste
- 1 cup/240 ml chicken broth, low sodium
- Zest of half a lemon

DIRECTIONS

1. Mix together lemon juice, olive oil, garlic, tarragon, salt, and pepper.
2. Place chicken in the crock pot and pour mixture over.
3. Add chicken broth and lemon zest.
4. Set on low and cook for 3.5 hours.
5. Serve warm, drizzling some of the sauce on top.

NUTRITION

- **Carbs: 4g**
- **Protein: 30g**
- **Fat: 8g**
- **Fiber: 0.5g**
- **Omega 3: 0.3g**
- **Vitamin D: 0.2μg**
- **Calcium: 15mg**
- **Iron: 1.2mg**

ALLERGENS & TIPS

Allergens: Chicken involved; ensure broth's allergen-free.

Tips: Use organic lemon for zest. Pair with steamed broccoli for a vitamin boost and more texture.

250 KCAL

2 SERVINGS

4 HOURS

CHICKEN RATATOUILLE

INGREDIENTS

- 2 chicken thighs (about 5 oz/140g each) – skinless, boneless
- 1 small zucchini (about 5 oz/140g), sliced
- 1 bell pepper (4 oz/115g), sliced
- Half an onion (2 oz/60g), chopped
- 1 tomato (4 oz/115g), diced
- 2 garlic cloves, finely minced
- ½ tsp/2.5 ml olive oil
- ¼ cup/60ml low-sodium chicken broth
- A pinch each of dried basil, thyme, and rosemary
- Salt and pepper, just a dash for taste!

NUTRITION

- **Carbs: 18g**
- **Protein: 28g**
- **Fat: 7g**
- **Fiber: 4g**
- **Omega 3: 0.1g**
- **Vitamin D: 0.3µg**
- **Calcium: 30mg**
- **Iron: 1.8mg**

DIRECTIONS

1. Combine zucchini, bell pepper, onion, tomato, garlic, herbs, olive oil, and chicken broth in the crock pot.
2. Nestle those chicken thighs right on top.
3. Season with salt and pepper.
4. Cover and set to low. Cook for about 4 hours.
5. Once done, give it a gentle mix and serve.

ALLERGENS & TIPS

Allergens: Contains chicken; watch the broth!

Tips: This pairs well with whole-grain toast. Plus, the longer it sits, the better the flavors meld. Leftovers? Yes, please!

HERBED CHICKEN AND LENTIL SOUP

230 KCAL

2 SERVINGS

5 HOURS

INGREDIENTS

- 2 chicken breasts (6 oz/170g each) – skinless
- ½ cup/115g dried lentils, rinsed
- 1 carrot (3 oz/85g), chopped
- 2 celery stalks (3 oz/85g), chopped
- ½ onion (2 oz/60g), diced
- 2 garlic cloves, minced
- 3 cups/710ml low-sodium chicken broth
- 1 tsp/5ml olive oil
- 1 tsp/5ml dried thyme
- 1 tsp/5ml dried rosemary
- Salt and pepper, to taste

NUTRITION

- **Carbs:** 25g
- **Protein:** 30g
- **Fat:** 4g
- **Fiber:** 10g
- **Omega 3:** 0.2g
- **Vitamin D:** 0.2µg
- **Calcium:** 35mg
- **Iron:** 3mg

DIRECTIONS

1. Add lentils, carrot, celery, onion, garlic, herbs, olive oil, and chicken broth into the crock pot.
2. Pop the chicken breasts on top.
3. Sprinkle with salt and pepper.
4. Cover and set on low. Cook for around 5 hours.
5. Once done, shred the chicken in the pot, stir, and enjoy.

ALLERGENS & TIPS

Allergens: Contains chicken (common allergen for some individuals) and lentils. Lentils are legumes; be cautious if you have peanut or other legume allergies.

Tips: This soup's flavor melds and becomes richer after sitting overnight. If you've got leftovers, they're perfect for a next-day treat. Adjust salt based on the broth's saltiness.

240 KCAL

2 SERVINGS

4 HOURS

TOMATO BASIL CHICKEN

INGREDIENTS

- 2 chicken breasts (6 oz/170g each)
- 1 can (14 oz/400g) diced tomatoes, drained
- ¼ cup/60ml fresh basil leaves, chopped
- 2 garlic cloves, minced
- ½ tsp/2.5ml olive oil
- Salt and pepper, to taste

DIRECTIONS

1. Drizzle olive oil at the base of your crock pot.
2. Layer in the chicken breasts. Season with a pinch of salt and pepper.
3. Scatter minced garlic over chicken.
4. Top chicken with the diced tomatoes and fresh basil.
5. Cover and cook on low for 4 hours until chicken is tender.
6. Serve with a sprinkle of fresh basil.

NUTRITION

- **Carbs: 8g**
- **Protein: 28g**
- **Fat: 5g**
- **Fiber: 2g**
- **Omega 3: 0.1g**
- **Vitamin D: 0.1µg**
- **Calcium: 40mg**
- **Iron: 1.2mg**

ALLERGENS & TIPS

Allergens: Contains chicken. Watch for tomato allergies, uncommon but can cause reactions in some.

Tips: For an enhanced taste, prep ingredients a night before, marinating them overnight.

CURRIED CHICKEN AND CAULIFLOWER

INGREDIENTS

- 2 chicken breasts (about 150g/5.3oz each)
- 2 cups cauliflower florets
- 1 medium onion, finely chopped
- 2 cloves garlic, minced
- 1 tbsp curry powder
- 1 tsp turmeric
- ½ cup chicken broth (120 ml)
- Salt & pepper to taste

NUTRITION

- **Carbs:** 14g
- **Protein:** 28g
- **Fat:** 5g
- **Fiber:** 4g
- **Omega 3:** 0.3g
- **Vitamin D:** 10% of Daily Intake
- **Calcium:** 40mg
- **Iron:** 2mg

DIRECTIONS

1. Mix curry powder, turmeric, salt, and pepper in a bowl.
2. Place chicken in the crock pot and rub the spice mix over it.
3. Add onions, garlic, and cauliflower on top.
4. Pour the chicken broth over the ingredients.
5. Cover and cook on low for 4 hours. Give it a gentle stir halfway if you can.
6. Serve hot. It's even better the next day if you save some leftovers.

ALLERGENS & TIPS

Allergens: Contains chicken. Ensure your curry mix is allergen-free; blends might contain nuts or dairy.

Tips: Its aroma gets stronger overnight, perfect for lunch the next day. Great for freezing and reheating, enhancing the flavors.

MOROCCAN TURKEY AND CHICKPEA STEW

320 KCAL
2 SERVINGS
4 HOURS

INGREDIENTS

- 1/2 lb (225g) lean turkey breast, cubed
- 1 can (15 oz/425g) chickpeas, drained
- 1 large tomato, diced
- 1/2 onion, finely chopped
- 1 garlic clove, minced
- 1 tsp ground cumin
- 1 tsp paprika
- 1/2 tsp turmeric
- Salt and pepper to taste
- 1 cup (240ml) low-sodium chicken broth
- 1 tbsp olive oil
- A handful of chopped cilantro for garnish

NUTRITION

- **Carbs: 40g**
- **Protein: 28g**
- **Fat: 10g**
- **Fiber: 8g**
- **Omega 3: 0.2g**
- **Vitamin D: 0 IU (minimal)**
- **Calcium: 90mg**
- **Iron: 3.6mg**

DIRECTIONS

1. In your crock pot, add turkey, chickpeas, tomato, onion, and garlic.
2. Mix in cumin, paprika, turmeric, salt, and pepper.
3. Pour in the chicken broth and drizzle with olive oil.
4. Cover and cook on low for 4 hours.
5. Serve hot, garnished with fresh cilantro.

ALLERGENS & TIPS

Allergens: Contains poultry and chickpeas; ensure spices are gluten-free.

Tips: You can sprinkle some feta on top for extra flavor. Also, let the stew sit overnight to boost its taste even more.

MAPLE-DIJON GLAZED TURKEY

310 KCAL
2 SERVINGS
4 HOURS

INGREDIENTS

- 1/2 lb (225g) turkey breast, sliced
- 2 tbsp pure maple syrup
- 1 tbsp Dijon mustard
- A pinch of sea salt and freshly ground pepper
- 1/2 tsp dried rosemary
- 1/2 cup (120ml) chicken broth (low-sodium, remember, we're keeping it healthy!)
- 1 tbsp olive oil (go for the extra virgin kind)

DIRECTIONS

1. First off, whisk together that sweet maple syrup and tangy Dijon mustard. Throw in the rosemary, salt, and pepper.
2. Lay out those turkey slices in your crock pot.
3. Drizzle the syrup-mustard mix over the turkey.
4. Gently pour in the chicken broth and top it off with olive oil.
5. Put the lid on, set it on low, and let it cook for 4 hours.
6. Once done, give yourself a pat on the back, and dig in!

NUTRITION

- **Carbs: 18g (mostly from that lovely maple!)**
- **Protein: 35g**
- **Fat: 8g**
- **Fiber: 0.5g**
- **Omega 3: 0.3g**
- **Vitamin D: 0 IU**
- **Calcium: 30mg**
- **Iron: 1.5mg**

ALLERGENS & TIPS

Allergens: Mustard might be an allergen for some folks.

Tips: Consider pairing this with some steamed greens or a light salad. And if you've got leftovers, it makes a fab sandwich filling!

TURKEY AND SWEET POTATO HASH

280 CAL
2 SERVINGS
3 HOURS

INGREDIENTS

- 1/2 lb (225g) lean turkey, minced
- 1 medium sweet potato, diced (roughly 1 cup or 150g)
- 1 onion, finely chopped
- 1 clove garlic, minced
- 1/2 tsp paprika
- 1 tbsp olive oil
- 1/4 cup (60ml) water
- Salt and pepper to taste

DIRECTIONS

1. Mix turkey, sweet potato, onion, and garlic in a bowl.
2. Add in paprika, and give it a good stir.
3. Transfer mixture to the crock pot.
4. Drizzle with olive oil and add water.
5. Season with salt and pepper.
6. Cover and cook on low for 3 hours until sweet potatoes are tender.

NUTRITION

- **Carbs: 20g**
- **Protein: 28g**
- **Fat: 6g**
- **Fiber: 3g**
- **Omega 3: 0.2g**
- **Vitamin D: 0 IU**
- **Calcium: 40mg**
- **Iron: 1.2mg**

ALLERGENS & TIPS

Allergens: Contains poultry. Always ensure turkey is thoroughly cooked.

Tips: Perfect with fresh coriander. A splash of lime livens it up. Remember, crock pot cooking times can vary. Keep an eye on the moisture levels, add a bit more water if needed.

TURKEY BOLOGNESE WITH ZUCCHINI NOODLES

330KCAL · 2 SERVINGS · 3 HOURS

INGREDIENTS

- ½ lb (225g) ground turkey
- 2 cups (500ml) crushed tomatoes
- 1 small onion, finely chopped
- 2 garlic cloves, minced
- 1 tbsp olive oil
- 1 tsp dried basil
- 1 tsp dried oregano
- Salt and pepper, to taste
- 2 large zucchinis, spiralized

DIRECTIONS

1. In your crock pot, combine turkey, tomatoes, onion, garlic, and spices.
2. Drizzle in the olive oil.
3. Cook on low for about 3 hours, stirring occasionally.
4. About 10 minutes before serving, add the zucchini noodles.
5. Allow them to heat through before dishing up.

NUTRITION

- **Carbs: 18g**
- **Protein: 28g**
- **Fat: 9g**
- **Fiber: 4g**
- **Omega 3: 0.3g**
- **Vitamin D: 10IU**
- **Calcium: 60mg**
- **Iron: 2.7mg**

ALLERGENS & TIPS

Allergens: Contains poultry.

Tips: The zoodles can get soft quick! Don't overcook. Add red pepper flakes if you're in the mood for a kick. Zoodles release water; you might want to drain a bit before serving.

ASIAN-INSPIRED TURKEY LETTUCE WRAPS

INGREDIENTS

- 1/2 pound (225g) lean ground turkey
- 2 tablespoons (30ml) low-sodium soy sauce
- 1 tablespoon (15ml) honey
- 1 teaspoon (5ml) sesame oil
- 1 small onion, diced
- 1 clove garlic, minced
- 4 large lettuce leaves (like iceberg or butterhead)
- 1 medium carrot, julienned
- 2 green onions, chopped for garnish

DIRECTIONS

1. Mix turkey, soy sauce, honey, sesame oil, onion, and garlic in the crock pot.
2. Cover and cook on low for 3-4 hours.
3. Once done, give it a good stir to break up the turkey into small pieces.
4. Spoon the cooked turkey mixture onto lettuce leaves.
5. Garnish with carrots and green onions. Wrap it up and munch away!

NUTRITION

- **Carbs:** 15g
- **Protein:** 25g
- **Fat:** 8g
- **Fiber:** 2g
- **Omega 3:** 0.2g
- **Vitamin D:** 10 IU
- **Calcium:** 35mg
- **Iron:** 2mg

ALLERGENS & TIPS

Allergens: Contains soy.

Tips: For added crunch, throw in some chopped water chestnuts or peanuts. Make sure to use low-sodium soy sauce to keep that salt in check.

290 KCAL

2 SERVINGS

4 HOURS

TURKEY AND KALE CHILI

INGREDIENTS

- 1/2 pound (225g) lean ground turkey
- 1 can (400g) diced tomatoes
- 1/2 cup (120ml) low-sodium chicken broth
- 1 cup (70g) kale, stemmed and torn into pieces
- 1 small onion, chopped
- 1 clove garlic, minced
- 1/2 teaspoon (2.5ml) cumin
- Pinch of chili flakes
- Salt and pepper, to taste

NUTRITION

- **Carbs: 18g**
- **Protein: 24g**
- **Fat: 5g**
- **Fiber: 4g**
- **Omega 3: 0.3g**
- **Vitamin D: 5 IU**
- **Calcium: 60mg**
- **Iron: 2.5mg**

DIRECTIONS

1. Brown the turkey in a pan, then transfer to the crock pot.
2. Toss in the tomatoes, chicken broth, onion, and garlic.
3. Season with cumin, chili flakes, salt, and pepper.
4. Cook on low for 3 hours.
5. Add the kale and let it simmer for an additional hour.
6. Stir well, adjust seasoning if needed, and serve warm.

ALLERGENS & TIPS

Allergens: Potential allergens based on chicken broth brand.

Tips: Great with a dollop of low-fat yogurt and a slice of whole-grain bread.

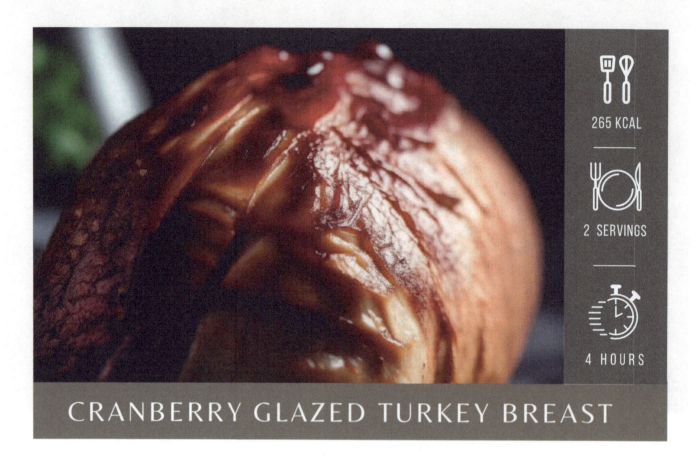

265 KCAL
2 SERVINGS
4 HOURS

CRANBERRY GLAZED TURKEY BREAST

INGREDIENTS

- Turkey breast: about 1/2 pound (225g)
- Fresh cranberries: 1/2 cup (55g)
- Pure maple syrup: 3 tablespoons (45ml)
- A dash of orange zest
- Ground cinnamon: 1/4 teaspoon (1.25ml)
- Salt and pepper: just a sprinkle, to taste!

DIRECTIONS

1. Mix cranberries, maple syrup, orange zest, and cinnamon in a bowl.
2. Season the turkey breast with salt and pepper.
3. Lay that turkey in your crock pot and pour the cranberry mixture over the top.
4. Set your pot to low and let it cook for about 4 hours.
5. When the turkey's all tender and glazed, it's chow time!

NUTRITION

- **Carbs: 30g**
- **Protein: 25g**
- **Fat: 3g**
- **Fiber: 2g**
- **Omega 3: 0.2g**
- **Vitamin D: 0 IU (Sorry, none here!)**
- **Calcium: 15mg**
- **Iron: 1.8mg**

ALLERGENS & TIPS

Allergens: Some folks can be sensitive to maple. Always read labels, alright?

Tips: Pssst! For a richer flavor, consider marinating overnight. Love a side? Roasted green beans pair beautifully. Leftovers? Makes scrumptious sandwiches!

PORK AND BROCCOLI CASSEROLE

320 KCAL
2 SERVINGS
4 HOURS

INGREDIENTS

- 8 oz (225 g) pork tenderloin, sliced thinly
- 2 cups (150 g) broccoli florets
- 1 onion, diced
- 1/2 cup (120 ml) chicken broth, low-sodium
- 2 cloves garlic, minced
- 1 tbsp (15 ml) olive oil
- Salt and pepper, to taste

DIRECTIONS

1. In your crock-pot, combine pork slices, broccoli, and onion.
2. Pour chicken broth over the mixture.
3. Stir in minced garlic, olive oil, salt, and pepper.
4. Cover and cook on low for 4 hours or until pork is tender and broccoli is cooked to your liking.
5. Serve hot and enjoy your hearty meal!

NUTRITION

- **Carbs: 18g**
- **Protein: 28g**
- **Fat: 10g**
- **Fiber: 4g**
- **Omega 3: 0.2g**
- **Vitamin D: 0.5µg**
- **Calcium: 60mg**
- **Iron: 1.8mg**

ALLERGENS & TIPS

Allergens: This dish contains pork. Ensure broth is allergen-free, or opt for homemade to control ingredients.

Tips: Pair with brown rice or quinoa for fiber. To enhance flavors, sear pork slices before adding to the crock-pot. Always source high-quality, lean pork for healthier results.

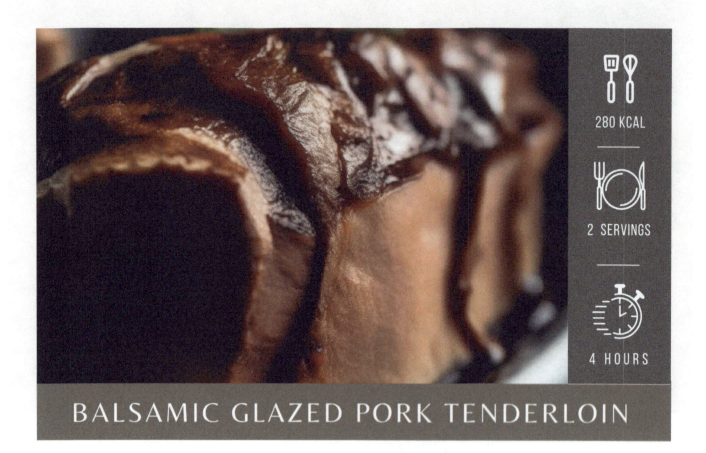

280 KCAL

2 SERVINGS

4 HOURS

BALSAMIC GLAZED PORK TENDERLOIN

INGREDIENTS

- Pork Tenderloin: 1/2 pound (225g)
- Balsamic Vinegar: 1/4 cup (60ml)
- Low-sodium Chicken Broth: 1/4 cup (60ml)
- Garlic Cloves (minced): 2
- Olive Oil: 1 tablespoon (15ml)
- Honey: 1 tablespoon (15ml)
- Dried Thyme: 1/2 teaspoon
- Dried Rosemary: 1/2 teaspoon
- Salt and Pepper: to taste

DIRECTIONS

1. Mix balsamic vinegar, chicken broth, minced garlic, honey, thyme, rosemary, and salt and pepper in a bowl.
2. Lightly brush the pork with olive oil. Place it into the crock-pot.
3. Pour the balsamic mixture over the pork.
4. Cover and cook on low for 4 hours, occasionally basting.
5. Once done, allow it to rest for a few minutes before slicing.

NUTRITION

- **Carbs:** 14g
- **Protein:** 30g
- **Fat:** 7g
- **Fiber:** 0.5g
- **Omega 3:** 0.2g
- **Vitamin D:** 1.2µg
- **Calcium:** 18mg
- **Iron:** 1.6mg

ALLERGENS & TIPS

Allergens: Verify honey and broth labels for potential allergens.

Tips: Try using aged balsamic for a deeper flavor. If the glaze is thin, reduce on stovetop post-cooking.

TUSCAN PORK AND BEAN SOUP

320 KCAL
2 SERVINGS
6 HOURS

INGREDIENTS

- Pork loin, cubed: 1/2 pound (225g)
- Cannellini beans, rinsed and drained: 1 cup (240ml)
- Low-sodium Vegetable Broth: 2 cups (480ml)
- Diced tomatoes: 1 cup (240ml)
- Garlic, minced: 1 clove
- Spinach leaves: 1/2 cup (120ml)
- Olive oil: 1 tsp (5ml)
- Italian herbs: 1 tsp
- Salt & pepper: to taste

DIRECTIONS

1. Heat olive oil in a pan. Brown the pork cubes lightly. Move them to the crock-pot.
2. Add beans, broth, tomatoes, garlic, and Italian herbs.
3. Cover. Let it cook on low for about 6 hours.
4. Stir in spinach in the last 15 minutes of cooking.
5. Season with salt and pepper. Serve hot!

NUTRITION

- **Carbs: 33g**
- **Protein: 28g**
- **Fat: 8g**
- **Fiber: 6g**
- **Omega 3: 0.4g**
- **Vitamin D: 0µg**
- **Calcium: 120mg**
- **Iron: 3.2mg**

ALLERGENS & TIPS

Allergens: Always check broth and beans for additional allergens, especially gluten.

Tips: Fresh spinach offers vibrant color. For a richer flavor, sprinkle with parmesan. Always adjust salt based on broth sodium content.

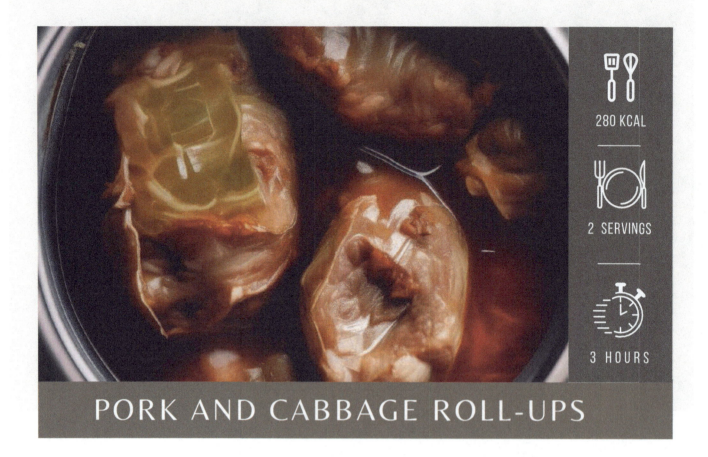

PORK AND CABBAGE ROLL-UPS

INGREDIENTS

- 2 pork loin fillets (about 6 oz each/170g)
- 4 cabbage leaves
- 1/2 onion, thinly sliced
- 1 garlic clove, minced
- 1/4 cup (60 ml) low-sodium chicken broth
- Salt and pepper, to taste
- 1 tsp (5 ml) olive oil

DIRECTIONS

1. Lay out your cabbage leaves and season your pork fillets with salt and pepper.
2. Place one pork fillet at the base of each cabbage leaf. Sprinkle some onion slices and garlic.
3. Roll up the cabbage leaves, keeping the pork snug inside.
4. Heat olive oil in a pan and brown roll-ups briefly.
5. Transfer roll-ups to the crock pot, pour in the chicken broth.
6. Cover and cook on low for about 3 hours or until pork is tender.

NUTRITION

- **Carbs:** 9g
- **Protein:** 29g
- **Fat:** 8g
- **Fiber:** 3g
- **Omega 3:** 0.2g
- **Vitamin D:** 0 IU (as pork loin doesn't contain significant Vitamin D)
- **Calcium:** 28mg
- **Iron:** 1.2mg

ALLERGENS & TIPS

Allergens: Contains garlic and onion. Ensure you're aware, especially if you or your guests have sensitivities.

Tips: Perfect with light gravy. Try a side of mashed potatoes or steamed veggies. Remember, slow cooking ensures flavor infusion and tender pork. Enjoy!

ROSEMARY ORANGE PORK ROAST

300 KCAL
2 SERVINGS
6 HOURS

INGREDIENTS

- Pork roast (about 1lb / 450g)
- 1 fresh orange, zested and juiced
- 1 tsp freshly chopped rosemary
- 2 cloves garlic, minced
- 1/2 tsp black pepper
- 1/2 tsp sea salt
- 1/4 cup water (60ml)
- 1 tbsp olive oil (15ml)

DIRECTIONS

1. Mix orange zest, juice, rosemary, garlic, pepper, and salt in a bowl.
2. Rub the mixture all over the pork roast.
3. Heat the olive oil in a pan and quickly sear each side of the roast.
4. Place the roast in the crockpot. Pour the water around it.
5. Set the crockpot on low. Cook for 5-6 hours or until the meat is tender.
6. Once done, let it rest for 10 minutes before slicing.

NUTRITION

- **Carbs: 8g**
- **Protein: 26g**
- **Fat: 10g**
- **Fiber: 1g**
- **Omega 3: 0.1g**
- **Vitamin D: 0.2mcg**
- **Calcium: 50mg**
- **Iron: 1.2mg**

ALLERGENS & TIPS

Allergens: Contains garlic. Do check for sensitivities.

Tips: Goes great with steamed greens. Fresh orange segments make a zesty garnish. Slow cooking lets the rosemary and orange meld beautifully.

290 KCAL

2 SERVINGS

4 HOURS

MAPLE-DIJON PORK CHOPS

INGREDIENTS

- 2 pork chops (about 6oz / 170g each)
- 3 tbsp maple syrup (45ml)
- 2 tbsp Dijon mustard (30ml)
- A pinch of sea salt
- 1/4 tsp black pepper
- 1 tbsp olive oil (15ml)
- 1/4 cup chicken broth (60ml)

NUTRITION

- **Carbs: 15g**
- **Protein: 25g**
- **Fat: 9g**
- **Fiber: 0.5g**
- **Omega 3: 0.2g**
- **Vitamin D: 0.3mcg**
- **Calcium: 60mg**
- **Iron: 1mg**

DIRECTIONS

1. Whisk together maple syrup and Dijon mustard. Add salt and pepper.
2. Coat pork chops in the mixture.
3. In a skillet, heat olive oil. Give those chops a quick sear.
4. Transfer pork chops to the crockpot. Pour chicken broth around them.
5. Cover. Cook on low for 3-4 hours. Kick back and enjoy your free time.

ALLERGENS & TIPS

Allergens: Contains mustard. Review all ingredient labels for potential allergens, especially if using store-bought broth or mustard with added ingredients.

Tips: Pairs wonderfully with steamed veggies. Maple glaze also works beautifully with chicken. Adjust crockpot times based on meat thickness

PORK WITH HERBED QUINOA

350 KCAL
2 SERVINGS
4 HOURS

INGREDIENTS

- Pork loin: 2 pieces (4 oz. each/113g)
- Quinoa: 1 cup (185g)
- Fresh herbs (basil, parsley, rosemary): 2 tbsp, chopped
- Chicken broth: 2 cups (475 ml)
- Olive oil: 1 tbsp (15 ml)
- Salt & pepper: to taste
- Lemon zest: 1 tsp

NUTRITION

- **Carbs: 45g**
- **Protein: 32g**
- **Fat: 9g**
- **Fiber: 5g**
- **Omega 3: 250mg**
- **Vitamin D: 1.2mcg**
- **Calcium: 32mg**
- **Iron: 2.8mg**

DIRECTIONS

1. Mix olive oil, salt, pepper, and lemon zest. Rub onto pork loins.
2. Place pork in the crock pot.
3. Pour chicken broth over pork.
4. Cook on low for 4 hours.
5. Around 15 minutes before serving, cook quinoa as per instructions.
6. Once done, fluff quinoa with a fork and stir in fresh herbs.
7. Serve pork over herbed quinoa.

ALLERGENS & TIPS

Allergens: No major allergens present. Always double-check quinoa packaging for cross-contaminants.

Tips: Perfect when paired with green salad. Leftover quinoa makes a refreshing cold salad for lunch!

300 KCAL

2 SERVINGS

6 HOURS

GARLIC-THYME BEEF STEW

INGREDIENTS

- Chopped beef cubes: 1/2 pound (227g)
- Baby potatoes, halved: 1 cup (150g)
- Carrots, sliced: 1 cup (130g)
- Fresh thyme: 1 tbsp (oh, that aroma!)
- Garlic cloves, minced: 2
- Beef broth: 1.5 cups (355 ml)
- Olive oil: 1 tsp (5 ml)
- Some good ol' salt & pepper to taste

DIRECTIONS

1. Give your beef a quick sear in that olive oil. Golden brown is what you're aiming for.
2. Toss everything - beef, potatoes, carrots, thyme, garlic, and that comforting broth - into the crock pot.
3. Season with salt & pepper.
4. Let it cook on low for 6-7 hours. The aroma? Intoxicating!

NUTRITION

- **Carbs: 30g**
- **Protein: 28g**
- **Fat: 8g**
- **Fiber: 4g**
- **Omega 3: 100mg**
- **Vitamin D: 0.8mcg**
- **Calcium: 40mg**
- **Iron: 3mg**

ALLERGENS & TIPS

Allergens: Contains beef. Ensure broth has no gluten or hidden allergens, especially if store-bought.

Tips: Leftovers taste richer the next day! Complement with a green salad to balance the meal. Consider using low-sodium broth for a healthier option. Fresh herbs can elevate flavors even more!

320 KCAL
2 SERVINGS
8 HOURS

ZESTY LEMON BEEF SKEWERS

INGREDIENTS

- 1/2 lb (227g) lean beef, cut into 1-inch cubes
- Zest and juice of 1 lemon
- 2 garlic cloves, minced
- 1 tbsp olive oil (cold-pressed)
- Pinch of red pepper flakes
- Salt & pepper to taste
- 4 wooden skewers, soaked in water

DIRECTIONS

1. Combine lemon zest, juice, garlic, olive oil, red pepper flakes, salt, and pepper in a bowl. Mix well.
2. Add beef cubes, ensuring they're coated. Cover and refrigerate for 4 hours.
3. Thread beef onto skewers evenly.
4. Place skewers in crock pot. Cook on low for 4 hours or until tender.

NUTRITION

- **Carbs:** 5g
- **Protein:** 28g
- **Fat:** 14g
- **Fiber:** 1g
- **Omega 3:** 0.3g
- **Vitamin D:** 1.2µg
- **Calcium:** 30mg
- **Iron:** 2.4m

ALLERGENS & TIPS

Allergens: Beef presence; check lemon zest/juice for additives if not using fresh.

Tips: Boost flavor by marinating overnight. To avoid drying out, keep a keen eye after 3 hours. Complement with steamed greens or a light quinoa salad. Enjoy the zesty undertones; they're a game-changer in this dish!

BEEF AND SPINACH CASSEROLE

380 KCAL
2 SERVINGS
4 HOURS

INGREDIENTS

- 200g (7oz) lean beef chunks
- 2 cups fresh spinach leaves
- 1 onion, chopped
- 1 garlic clove, minced
- ½ cup (120ml) low-sodium beef broth
- 1 tsp olive oil
- ½ tsp dried basil
- ½ tsp dried oregano
- Salt and pepper to taste

NUTRITION

- **Carbs: 10g**
- **Protein: 35g**
- **Fat: 12g**
- **Fiber: 3g**
- **Omega 3: 0.5g**
- **Vitamin D: 0 IU**
- **Calcium: 80mg**
- **Iron: 3mg**

DIRECTIONS

1. In a pan, quickly sear beef chunks in olive oil until browned.
2. Transfer beef to the crock pot.
3. Add in onion, garlic, broth, and seasonings.
4. Cover and cook on low for about 3 hours.
5. Toss in fresh spinach and stir gently.
6. Continue cooking for another hour or until beef is tender.
7. Taste and adjust seasoning before serving.

ALLERGENS & TIPS

Allergens: Contains beef. Check broth for potential allergens.

Tips: Pair with crusty bread. For crisper spinach, stir it in closer to the end. Always use fresh produce for best flavor and health benefits.

LEMON-PEPPER BEEF STEAKS

INGREDIENTS

- 2 beef steaks (about 6 oz. / 170g each)
- 1 large lemon, juiced and zested
- 2 tsp (10 ml) black pepper, freshly ground
- 1/2 cup (120 ml) beef broth, low sodium
- 2 cloves garlic, minced
- 1 tbsp (15 ml) olive oil
- Salt, to taste

DIRECTIONS

1. Drizzle olive oil over the beef steaks, ensuring they're well-coated.
2. Season each steak generously with freshly ground black pepper.
3. In your crock pot, combine beef broth, lemon juice, zest, and minced garlic.
4. Place the beef steaks into the mixture. Ensure they're well submerged.
5. Cover and cook on low for about 2 hours until they're tender and well-cooked.
6. Season with salt, if needed, and serve hot.

NUTRITION

- **Carbs: 5g**
- **Protein: 30g**
- **Fat: 11g**
- **Fiber: 1g**
- **Omega 3: 0.4g**
- **Vitamin D: 1.2µg**
- **Calcium: 20mg**
- **Iron: 2.1mg**

ALLERGENS & TIPS

Allergens: Contains beef. Always check broth labels for any unexpected allergens.

Tips: For added zing, marinate steaks in lemon zest for 30 minutes before cooking. If you prefer it medium-rare, check at 1.5 hours! Enjoy with a side salad!

BEEF, CABBAGE, AND CARROT SOUP

INGREDIENTS

- 200g (7 oz.) beef chunks
- 1/2 cabbage, chopped
- 2 carrots, sliced
- 3 cups (710 ml) beef broth, low sodium
- 1 tsp olive oil
- Salt and pepper, to taste
- Fresh herbs (like parsley), optional

DIRECTIONS

1. In your crock pot, pour the beef broth.
2. Add in the beef chunks, cabbage, and sliced carrots.
3. Drizzle with that little bit of olive oil.
4. Sprinkle in some salt and pepper. You know, for that flavor kick.
5. Turn it on low, let it do its thing for 3 hours.
6. Once done, give it a good stir. Garnish with fresh herbs if you fancy.

NUTRITION

- **Carbs: 12g**
- **Protein: 18g**
- **Fat: 5g**
- **Fiber: 3g**
- **Omega 3: 0.2g**
- **Vitamin D: 1.0µg**
- **Calcium: 40mg**
- **Iron: 2.5mg**

ALLERGENS & TIPS

Allergens: Contains beef. Double-check the broth for any potential allergens.

Tips: For a thicker soup, consider blending half the mixture after cooking. And hey, a dash of hot sauce never hurt anyone. Enjoy warm with some crusty bread.

250 KCAL
2 SERVINGS
4 HOURS

BEEF AND BUTTERNUT SQUASH STEW

INGREDIENTS

- 150g (5.3 oz.) lean beef, diced
- 1 small butternut squash, peeled & cubed
- 2 cups (475 ml) vegetable broth, low sodium
- 1 onion, diced
- 1 garlic clove, minced
- 1/2 tsp thyme
- 1/2 tsp rosemary
- Salt and pepper, to taste

DIRECTIONS

1. Toss that beef into your crock pot. Look at you go!
2. Add your butternut squash cubes. They're the star after all.
3. Now, throw in the onions and minced garlic. Smells good, right?
4. Time for some aromatic herbs! Add thyme, rosemary, and season with salt & pepper.
5. Pour in that vegetable broth. We're making magic here.
6. Cover and cook on low for about 4 hours. When it's tender and flavorful, you'll know it's done.

NUTRITION

- **Carbs: 30g**
- **Protein: 20g**
- **Fat: 6g**
- **Fiber: 5g**
- **Omega 3: 0.3g**
- **Vitamin D: 1.5µg**
- **Calcium: 75mg**
- **Iron: 3mg**

ALLERGENS & TIPS

Allergens: Contains beef.

Tips: Want a bit more kick? A pinch of paprika does wonders. Also, serve with a slice of whole grain bread to soak up the goodness. Happy eating!

320 KCAL
2 SERVINGS
3 HOURS

BEEF AND VEGETABLE RATATOUILLE

INGREDIENTS

- 150g (5.3 oz.) lean beef chunks
- 1 zucchini, sliced
- 1 bell pepper, chopped
- 1 tomato, diced
- 2 cups (475 ml) tomato sauce, low sodium
- 1 onion, chopped
- 2 cloves garlic, minced
- Salt and a dash of black pepper
- Sprinkle of dried basil and oregano

NUTRITION

- **Carbs: 25g**
- **Protein: 23g**
- **Fat: 7g**
- **Fiber: 6g**
- **Omega 3: 0.2g**
- **Vitamin D: 1µg**
- **Calcium: 50mg**
- **Iron: 2.5mg**

DIRECTIONS

1. Layer beef at the bottom of the crock pot.
2. Top with zucchini, bell pepper, and tomato.
3. Scatter onions and garlic over the veggies.
4. Pour the tomato sauce, covering everything nicely.
5. Season with salt, pepper, basil, and oregano.
6. Close the lid. Cook on low for 5 hours. Give it a stir halfway if you like.

ALLERGENS & TIPS

Allergens: Contains beef. Check tomato sauce for potential allergens; some might contain dairy or gluten.

Tips: Use organically grown veggies for richer flavor. A splash of red wine can add depth. Always cool leftovers rapidly and refrigerate. Perfect reheated the next day for a tasty lunch!

TUSCAN LAMB AND ARTICHOKE STEW

310 KCAL
2 SERVINGS
4 HOURS

INGREDIENTS

- Lamb pieces: 300g (10.5 oz)
- Artichoke hearts: 6, quartered
- Diced tomatoes: 1 can (400g/14 oz)
- Garlic cloves: 2, minced
- Fresh rosemary: 1 sprig
- Low-sodium vegetable broth: 2 cups (475 ml)
- Olive oil: 1 tbsp (15 ml)
- Salt and pepper: to taste

NUTRITION

- **Carbs: 22g**
- **Protein: 28g**
- **Fat: 12g**
- **Fiber: 6g**
- **Omega 3: 0.2g**
- **Vitamin D: 1.5µg**
- **Calcium: 55mg**
- **Iron: 3.8mg**

DIRECTIONS

1. In your crockpot, layer the lamb pieces at the bottom.
2. Spread the quartered artichoke hearts evenly over the lamb.
3. Sprinkle minced garlic, and then pour in the diced tomatoes, juice and all.
4. Tuck that fresh rosemary sprig in. It'll do wonders, trust me.
5. Add in vegetable broth, and drizzle with olive oil.
6. Season with a pinch of salt and a dash of pepper.
7. Cover and let it simmer on low for 4 hours until the lamb is tender.

ALLERGENS & TIPS

Allergens: Contains lamb. Double-check canned goods for potential additives.

Tips: Go for fresh artichokes if in season; they elevate the stew. Serve with a whole grain roll for a complete cozy meal.

LAMB AND ASPARAGUS STIR FRY

320 KCAL
2 SERVINGS
3 HOURS

INGREDIENTS

- Lamb strips: 250g (8.8 oz)
- Fresh asparagus: 200g (7 oz), cut into thirds
- Soy sauce (low-sodium): 2 tbsp (30 ml)
- Garlic cloves: 2, finely chopped
- Ginger: 1 tsp, minced
- Olive oil: 1 tsp (5 ml)
- Water: 1/2 cup (120 ml)
- Pepper: a sprinkle

NUTRITION

- **Carbs: 10g**
- **Protein: 24g**
- **Fat: 10g**
- **Fiber: 3g**
- **Omega 3: 0.1g**
- **Vitamin D: 0.6µg**
- **Calcium: 30mg**
- **Iron: 2.8mg**

DIRECTIONS

1. In your trusty crockpot, place lamb strips.
2. Add asparagus pieces next.
3. Mix soy sauce, garlic, and ginger in a bowl. Pour this mix over the lamb and asparagus.
4. Drizzle olive oil, ensuring everything gets a bit of shine.
5. Add water for a bit of steam magic. Season with pepper.
6. Close the lid, set on low, and give it a 3-hour slow dance.

ALLERGENS & TIPS

Allergens: Contains soy. Ensure lamb source is clear of additives.

Tips: Lightly toast sesame seeds and sprinkle on top before serving. Gives a lovely crunch!

275 KCAL

2 SERVINGS

6 HOURS

LAMB WITH CILANTRO AND LIME

INGREDIENTS

- Lamb shoulder: 300g (10.5 oz)
- Fresh cilantro: A handful, chopped
- Lime: Zest and juice of 1
- Olive oil: 1 tbsp (15 ml) - the good kind!
- Garlic: 2 cloves, minced
- Ground cumin: 1 tsp
- Salt & pepper: To taste
- Water: 1/4 cup (60 ml)

DIRECTIONS

1. First, mix that vibrant cilantro, zesty lime, aromatic garlic, and earthy cumin in a bowl.
2. Drizzle your lamb with that fancy olive oil, then rub in your cilantro mixture.
3. Pop the lamb into the crockpot.
4. Pour in the water and season with salt & pepper.
5. Close the lid, set on low, and let it simmer to perfection for 4 hours.

NUTRITION

- **Carbs:** 5g
- **Protein:** 28g
- **Fat:** 12g
- **Fiber:** 0.5g
- **Omega 3:** 0.2g
- **Vitamin D:** 1µg
- **Calcium:** 20mg
- **Iron:** 3mg

ALLERGENS & TIPS

Allergens: Garlic might upset sensitive stomachs.

Tips: Garnish with extra fresh cilantro leaves and a lime wedge. It's all about the presentation, right?

LAMB AND EGGPLANT RAGOUT

INGREDIENTS

- About 200g (7 oz) lean lamb chunks. The leaner, the better.
- 1 decent-sized eggplant, cubed
- 1 can (14 oz) diced tomatoes. The juicier, the better.
- 2 garlic cloves, minced (love that aroma!)
- 1 onion, finely chopped
- A pinch or two of rosemary
- 1/4 cup (60 ml) chicken broth. Or vegetable, if you're feeling adventurous.
- A sprinkle of salt & pepper. As per your taste.
- A tad of olive oil, roughly 1 tbsp (15 ml).

DIRECTIONS

1. Warm up that olive oil in a pan and get that lamb golden brown. Like a tan!
2. Into the crockpot they go.
3. Add eggplant, tomatoes, garlic, onion. A lovely mix.
4. Season with rosemary, salt, pepper.
5. Pour the broth over it and mix well.
6. Lid on, set on low. Let the magic brew for 6 hours.

NUTRITION

- **Carbs: 20g**
- **Protein: 22g**
- **Fat: 8g (the good kind!)**
- **Fiber: 5g**
- **Omega 3: 0.3g**
- **Vitamin D: 0.5µg**
- **Calcium: 40mg**
- **Iron: 2.8mg**

ALLERGENS & TIPS

Allergens: Contains lamb. Not veggie-friendly, folks! Also, those with tomato allergies or intolerances should take caution.

Tips: Consider fresh parsley on top. It's like a touch of nature on your plate.

LAMB WITH ROASTED RED PEPPER SAUCE

280 KCAL
2 SERVINGS
6 HOURS

INGREDIENTS

- 200g (7 oz) lean lamb, sliced into thin strips
- 2 roasted red peppers, chopped
- 1 garlic clove, minced
- 1/2 onion, diced
- 1/2 cup (120 ml) low-sodium beef broth
- 1 tbsp (15 ml) olive oil
- Salt and pepper, to taste

NUTRITION

- **Carbs:** 12g
- **Protein:** 25g
- **Fat:** 10g
- **Fiber:** 2g
- **Omega 3:** 0.2g
- **Vitamin D:** 0.4μg
- **Calcium:** 28mg
- **Iron:** 2.5mg

DIRECTIONS

1. Start off by heating the olive oil in a pan. Toss in the lamb strips and give them a quick sear until they're just brown.
2. Place the seared lamb in your crock pot.
3. Now, let's get saucy! Combine roasted red peppers, garlic, and onion in a blender. Whizz it up until you've got a smooth blend.
4. Pour that delightful sauce over the lamb in the crock pot. Add in the beef broth.
5. Season with salt and pepper.
6. Close the lid, set to low, and let it simmer for 6 hours. Patience is key!

ALLERGENS & TIPS

Allergens: This dish contains lamb. Potential allergens might be present based on the broth brand. Ensure to always check ingredient labels for undisclosed items.

Tips: Serve with steamed green beans or asparagus. A splash of lemon juice before serving? Heaven!

GREEK-INSPIRED LAMB AND OLIVE STEW

450 KCAL
2 SERVINGS
4 HOURS

INGREDIENTS

- 1/2 pound (227 grams) lamb cubes
- 1 cup (240 mL) chicken broth, low sodium
- 1/4 cup (60 mL) green olives, pitted
- 1 onion, chopped
- 2 garlic cloves, minced
- 1/4 cup (60 mL) diced tomatoes
- 1 tsp dried oregano
- Salt and pepper to taste

NUTRITION

- **Carbs: 20g**
- **Protein: 25g**
- **Fat: 20g**
- **Fiber: 3g**
- **Omega 3: 0.5g**
- **Vitamin D: 1.5μg**
- **Calcium: 45mg**
- **Iron: 3mg**

DIRECTIONS

1. Combine lamb, onion, and garlic in the crock pot.
2. Stir in chicken broth, diced tomatoes, oregano, salt, and pepper.
3. Cook on low for 3.5 hours.
4. Add green olives, then cook for another 30 minutes.
5. Serve hot, ideally with a side of quinoa or whole grain bread.

ALLERGENS & TIPS

Allergens: Contains lamb. Broth may have allergens; check the label.

Tips: Best served with a fresh Greek salad. Leftovers taste even better the next day.

LAMB AND LENTIL STEW

420 KCAL
2 SERVINGS
6 HOURS

INGREDIENTS

- 8 oz (227 grams) lean lamb, cubed
- 1/2 cup (115 grams) lentils, washed and drained
- 1 small onion, diced
- 2 garlic cloves, minced
- 2 cups (480 mL) vegetable broth
- 1 carrot, sliced
- 1/2 tsp cumin
- Salt and pepper, a pinch
- Fresh parsley, for garnish

NUTRITION

- **Carbs: 35g**
- **Protein: 28g**
- **Fat: 8g**
- **Fiber: 10g**
- **Omega 3: 0.2g**
- **Vitamin D: 0.8µg**
- **Calcium: 60mg**
- **Iron: 5mg**

DIRECTIONS

1. Add lamb, lentils, onion, and garlic to the crock pot.
2. Pour in vegetable broth, ensuring the ingredients are submerged.
3. Mix in carrot slices, cumin, salt, and pepper.
4. Cover and set to low for 6 hours.
5. Serve with a sprinkle of fresh parsley on top.

ALLERGENS & TIPS

Allergens: Contains lamb. Beware if you're sensitive to legumes.

Tips: Pair with a side salad for a fresh touch. Cooked stew can be stored in the fridge for up to 2 days

350 KCAL

2 SERVINGS

2 HOURS

COD WITH LEMON AND DILL SAUCE

INGREDIENTS

- 2 fresh cod fillets (about 6 oz or 170 grams each)
- 1 lemon, zested and juiced
- 2 tsp (10 mL) olive oil
- A handful of fresh dill, chopped
- 1 garlic clove, crushed
- Salt & pepper, to taste
- 1/2 cup (120 mL) low-fat yogurt

DIRECTIONS

1. Place your beautiful cod fillets in the crock pot.
2. Mix together the lemon zest, juice, olive oil, dill, and garlic in a bowl. Drizzle this magic mixture over the cod.
3. Cover and cook on low for 2 hours.
4. Before serving, whisk the yogurt into the pot to create that creamy dill sauce.

NUTRITION

- **Carbs:** 8g
- **Protein:** 40g
- **Fat:** 8g
- **Fiber:** 1g
- **Omega 3:** 1.5g
- **Vitamin D:** 3.2µg
- **Calcium:** 150mg
- **Iron:** 0.8mg

ALLERGENS & TIPS

Allergens: Contains fish and dairy (yogurt).

Tips: Serve with steamed veggies to boost nutrients. The sauce? It's also awesome over potatoes!

320 KCAL
2 SERVINGS
3 HOURS

SHRIMP AND VEGETABLE CURRY

INGREDIENTS

- 1/2 lb (225 grams) fresh shrimp, peeled and deveined
- 1 cup (240 mL) mixed vegetables (like bell peppers, broccoli, and carrots)
- 1 can (14 oz or 400 mL) light coconut milk
- 2 tsp (10 mL) curry powder
- 1 onion, chopped
- 1 garlic clove, minced
- 1/2 tsp (2.5 mL) ginger, grated
- Salt & pepper, for seasoning
- 1 tsp (5 mL) olive oil

NUTRITION

- **Carbs: 20g**
- **Protein: 24g**
- **Fat: 9g**
- **Fiber: 5g**
- **Omega 3: 1g**
- **Vitamin D: 1.5µg**
- **Calcium: 80mg**
- **Iron: 2mg**

DIRECTIONS

1. In the crock pot, heat olive oil and add onion, garlic, and ginger. Let them mingle.
2. Throw in the mixed veggies, giving them a good stir.
3. Pour in the coconut milk, stir in curry powder, and season with salt & pepper.
4. Add the shrimp on top and cover.
5. Cook on low for 3 hours, until shrimp is pink and veggies are tender.

ALLERGENS & TIPS

Allergens: Contains shrimp, coconut. Those allergic to shellfish or tree nuts should avoid or seek alternatives.

Tips: Brown rice pairs beautifully with this curry, adding essential fiber. Flavor deepens with time, making leftovers even more delightful. Adjust spices as desired, making the dish your own culinary masterpiece.

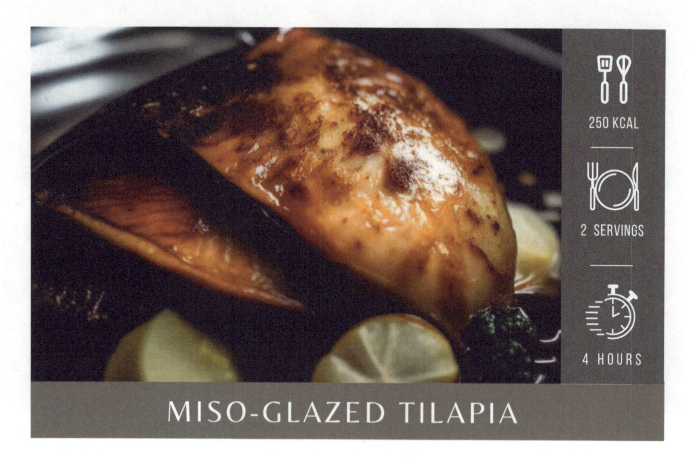

MISO-GLAZED TILAPIA

250 KCAL
2 SERVINGS
4 HOURS

INGREDIENTS

- 2 Tilapia fillets (6 oz/170g each)
- 2 tbsp white miso paste
- 1 tbsp honey
- 1 tbsp soy sauce
- 1 tsp ginger, freshly grated
- 1 garlic clove, minced
- 2 green onions, finely chopped
- Juice of half a lemon

DIRECTIONS

1. In a bowl, whisk together miso paste, honey, soy sauce, ginger, garlic, and lemon juice.
2. Coat Tilapia fillets with the miso mixture, ensuring even coverage.
3. Place the fillets in the crockpot.
4. Cook on LOW for 3-4 hours.
5. Once done, sprinkle with green onions.

NUTRITION

- **Carbs:** 15g
- **Protein:** 28g
- **Fat:** 7g
- **Fiber:** 1g
- **Omega 3:** 250mg
- **Vitamin D:** 100 IU
- **Calcium:** 30mg
- **Iron:** 0.8mg

ALLERGENS & TIPS

Allergens: Contains fish, soy.

Tips: Pair with steamed veggies for a balanced meal. Opt for wild-caught Tilapia if possible. The longer marination, the richer the flavors. Adjust miso if a lighter taste is desired.

320 KCAL

2 SERVINGS

4.5 HOURS

SEAFOOD PAELLA WITH SAFFRON

INGREDIENTS

- 1 cup (240g) short-grain rice
- 2 cups (475ml) chicken broth
- 4 oz (115g) shrimp, peeled
- 4 oz (115g) mussels, cleaned
- 2 oz (60g) calamari rings
- 1 pinch of saffron threads
- 1 onion, chopped
- 2 garlic cloves, minced
- 1 bell pepper, sliced
- 2 tbsp olive oil
- 1 tsp paprika
- Salt & pepper to taste
- Lemon wedges for serving
- Fresh parsley, chopped

NUTRITION

- **Carbs: 48g**
- **Protein: 22g**
- **Fat: 10g**
- **Fiber: 3g**
- **Omega 3: 120mg**
- **Vitamin D: 45 IU**
- **Calcium: 50mg**
- **Iron: 2mg**

DIRECTIONS

1. Start by heating olive oil in a skillet. Toss in onion, garlic, and bell pepper. Sauté until softened.
2. Transfer veggies to the crockpot, followed by rice, saffron, paprika, salt, pepper, and chicken broth.
3. Cover and set to LOW. Let it cook for 4 hours.
4. Add in shrimp, mussels, and calamari. Stir gently. Continue cooking for another 30 minutes.
5. Before serving, sprinkle parsley and accompany with lemon wedges.

ALLERGENS & TIPS

Allergens: Contains seafood, shellfish.

Tips: Use fresh seafood for best flavors. Make sure mussels open during cooking; discard any that don't. Feel free to customize with your favorite seafood.

280 KCAL
2 SERVINGS
4 HOURS

CLAM AND CORN CHOWDER

INGREDIENTS

- 6 oz (170g) clams, cleaned
- 1 cup (240g) corn kernels
- 1 medium potato, diced
- 2 cups (475ml) vegetable broth
- ½ cup (120ml) light cream
- 1 onion, chopped
- 2 garlic cloves, minced
- 1 celery stalk, sliced
- 1 tbsp olive oil
- Salt & pepper to taste
- Fresh chives for garnish

DIRECTIONS

1. Heat up that olive oil in a skillet, toss in the onion, garlic, and celery. Once they're all golden and smelling amazing, transfer them into the crockpot.
2. Now, throw in the potatoes, clams, corn, and vegetable broth.
3. Season with a pinch of salt and pepper. Give it a good mix, ensuring everything's cozy in there.
4. Put the lid on and set your crockpot on LOW for 3 hours.
5. Once done, stir in the light cream. Let it mingle for another 20 minutes.
6. Serve piping hot and don't forget to sprinkle some chives on top for that extra zing!

NUTRITION

- **Carbs: 40g**
- **Protein: 15g**
- **Fat: 8g**
- **Fiber: 5g**
- **Omega 3: 100mg**
- **Vitamin D: 30 IU**
- **Calcium: 70mg**
- **Iron: 1.5mg**

ALLERGENS & TIPS

Allergens: Contains shellfish, dairy.

Tips: Opt for fresh clams for a richer taste. And if you're feeling adventurous, maybe sprinkle a bit of smoked paprika before serving.

HERBED HALIBUT AND GREEN BEANS

260 KCAL
2 SERVINGS
3 HOURS

INGREDIENTS

- 2 halibut fillets (6 oz or 170g each)
- 1 ½ cups (150g) fresh green beans, trimmed
- 2 tsp olive oil
- 1 lemon, zested and juiced
- 1 tsp dried thyme
- 1 tsp dried rosemary
- Salt & pepper, to taste
- 2 garlic cloves, minced
- ½ cup (120ml) low-sodium chicken broth

DIRECTIONS

1. Mix olive oil, lemon zest, juice, thyme, rosemary, garlic, salt, and pepper in a bowl. This is your flavor bomb right here.
2. Toss halibut fillets in the herby mixture, ensuring they're nicely coated.
3. Place green beans at the bottom of the crockpot. Lay the halibut on top.
4. Pour chicken broth over everything. It's all about keeping it juicy.
5. Set your crockpot on LOW. Let it all mingle for about 2.5 hours.
6. Check for doneness. Once the fish flakes easily with a fork, you're good to go!

NUTRITION

- **Carbs: 10g**
- **Protein: 32g**
- **Fat: 8g**
- **Fiber: 4g**
- **Omega 3: 1200mg**
- **Vitamin D: 570 IU**
- **Calcium: 56mg**
- **Iron: 1.2mg**

ALLERGENS & TIPS

Allergens: Contains fish.

Tips: For an added kick, sprinkle some crushed red pepper. Choose fresh green beans for the best flavo

SEAFOOD JAMBALAYA

280 KCAL

2 SERVINGS

4 HOURS

INGREDIENTS

- ½ cup (95g) long-grain rice
- ½ lb (225g) mixed seafood (like shrimp and mussels)
- 1 small onion, diced
- 1 bell pepper, chopped
- 1 garlic clove, minced
- 1 can (14 oz or 400g) diced tomatoes
- ½ tsp paprika
- ½ tsp cayenne (keep it spicy!)
- Salt & pepper, to taste
- 1 cup (240ml) low-sodium vegetable broth

DIRECTIONS

1. Here's what you'll do first - mix those veggies, garlic, and spices in the crockpot.
2. Next, pour in that mouthwatering can of diced tomatoes and vegetable broth.
3. Stir in the rice. Give everything a nice mix.
4. Now, add in the seafood on top.
5. Set the crockpot on LOW and let it cook for around 3.5 hours.
6. Once the rice is soft and the seafood is cooked through, you're ready to feast!

NUTRITION

- **Carbs: 45g**
- **Protein: 18g**
- **Fat: 5g**
- **Fiber: 4g**
- **Omega 3: 800mg**
- **Vitamin D: 80 IU**
- **Calcium: 60mg**
- **Iron: 2.5mg**

ALLERGENS & TIPS

Allergens: Contains seafood.

Tips: Got some fresh herbs? Toss them in last minute for added flair. Always opt for sustainable seafood.

HEARTY VEGETABLE AND BEAN SOUP

275 KCAL
2 SERVINGS
4 HOURS

INGREDIENTS

- 1 cup of mixed beans (like kidney, black, and navy), soaked overnight
- 2 large carrots, chopped
- 1 celery stalk, diced
- 1 onion, finely sliced
- 2 garlic cloves, minced
- 4 cups vegetable broth (960 ml)
- 1 tsp olive oil
- Salt and pepper to taste
- 1 tsp dried oregano
- 1 bay leaf

DIRECTIONS

1. Drizzle olive oil in the crock pot. Toss in garlic and onions; let them sizzle a bit.
2. Pour in vegetable broth.
3. Toss in the beans, carrots, and celery. Stir them up a bit.
4. Season with salt, pepper, oregano, and add the bay leaf.
5. Cover and cook on low for 4 hours, stirring occasionally.
6. Taste, adjust the seasoning if needed, and enjoy the warmth!

NUTRITION

- **Carbs: 45g**
- **Protein: 14g**
- **Fat: 3g**
- **Fiber: 10g**
- **Omega 3: 0.4g**
- **Vitamin D: 0 IU (none present)**
- **Calcium: 90mg**
- **Iron: 3mg**

ALLERGENS & TIPS

Allergens: Contains beans (a potential allergen for some).

Tips: Best enjoyed with crusty bread or a side salad!

EGGPLANT AND TOMATO RATATOUILLE

230 KCAL
2 SERVINGS
4 HOURS

INGREDIENTS

- Eggplant, 1 medium-sized, cubed
- Tomatoes, 2, diced (that's about 200g)
- 1 bell pepper, sliced
- Onion, 1, chopped
- Garlic cloves, 2, minced
- 2 tsp olive oil (around 10 ml)
- Fresh basil, a handful, torn
- A pinch of salt and pepper

DIRECTIONS

1. Start with your crock pot. Put the olive oil, onion, and garlic. Let them make friends for a bit.
2. Now, add the eggplant, tomatoes, and bell pepper.
3. Season with salt and pepper, give it a good stir.
4. Lid on, let it simmer on low for about 4 hours.
5. When it's nearly done, sprinkle that fresh basil on top. Voilà!

NUTRITION

- **Carbs:** 35g
- **Protein:** 5g
- **Fat:** 8g
- **Fiber:** 9g
- **Omega 3:** 0.3g
- **Vitamin D:** 0 IU
- **Calcium:** 40mg
- **Iron:** 1.8mg

ALLERGENS & TIPS

Allergens: None.

Tips: Ratatouille's flavor deepens overnight. Consider making ahead and reheating for best taste.

SPINACH AND FETA STUFFED PORTOBELLOS

210 KCAL • 2 SERVINGS • 3 HOURS

INGREDIENTS

- 2 big Portobello mushrooms, gently cleaned.
- Spinach, 200g or 7oz, fresh is best!
- Feta cheese, 50g or 1.7oz, crumbled up.
- A tiny onion, finely chopped.
- A hint of olive oil, 1 tsp or 5ml.
- A sprinkle of black pepper & salt

NUTRITION

- **Carbs: 12g**
- **Protein: 8g**
- **Fat: 14g**
- **Fiber: 2g**
- **Omega 3: 0.1g**
- **Vitamin D: 0.5µg**
- **Calcium: 150mg**
- **Iron: 2.5mg**

DIRECTIONS

1. Wipe away any dirt from the Portobellos using a damp paper towel. Remove the stems. If you fancy a deeper cup for filling, gently scrape out some of the gills using a spoon. But hey, that's optional.
2. In a bowl, mix together the fresh spinach, crumbled feta, finely chopped onion, a dash of salt, and a sprinkle of black pepper. Stir it up until everything's good friends.
3. Stuff Them Up: Time to get those Portobellos packed. Take generous scoops of your spinach mix and fill the mushroom caps. Press down gently, we want it snug.
4. Before they hit the crock pot, drizzle them with that olive oil. Helps them stay moist and adds a touch of flavor.
5. Carefully place your stuffed mushrooms in the crock pot. No need to stack, let them have their space. Set the crock pot to low, and let it work its magic for about 3 hours.
6. After 3 hours, those mushrooms should be tender and the filling hot and melded. Carefully scoop them out, plate, and get ready for a treat!

ALLERGENS & TIPS

Allergens: Contains dairy (feta).

Tips: Try a balsamic glaze drizzle post-cooking for a flavor pop!

CAULIFLOWER AND CHICKPEA TIKKA MASALA

INGREDIENTS

- 1 small cauliflower, chopped (1 lb / 450g)
- 1 cup chickpeas, rinsed and drained (15 oz / 425g can)
- 1 cup tikka masala sauce (240ml)
- 1/2 cup water (120ml)
- 1/2 tsp ground turmeric
- Salt, to taste
- Fresh cilantro, for garnish

NUTRITION

- **Carbs: 34g**
- **Protein: 9g**
- **Fat: 4g**
- **Fiber: 8g**
- **Omega 3: 0.1g**
- **Vitamin D: Negligible**
- **Calcium: 75mg**
- **Iron: 2.5mg**

DIRECTIONS

1. Combine cauliflower, chickpeas, tikka masala sauce, water, and turmeric in the crock pot.
2. Stir well, ensuring all ingredients are coated.
3. Cook on low for 3 hours.
4. Season with salt and garnish with cilantro before serving.

ALLERGENS & TIPS

Allergens: Chickpeas are legumes. Be cautious if allergic.

Tips: Sautéing spices enhances flavor, fresh cilantro offers a refreshing contrast, pair with brown rice for a balanced meal.

SWEET POTATO AND BLACK BEAN CHILI

320 KCAL • 2 SERVINGS • 3 HOURS

INGREDIENTS

- 1 large sweet potato, diced (about 1.5 cups)
- 1 can (15 oz.) black beans, drained and rinsed
- 1 can (14 oz.) diced tomatoes, with juice
- 1 red bell pepper, chopped
- 1/2 onion, chopped
- 2 cloves garlic, minced
- 1 tsp cumin
- 1/2 tsp chili powder
- 1/4 tsp paprika
- Salt & pepper to taste
- 2 cups vegetable broth (16 fl oz/475 ml)

NUTRITION

- **Carbs: 60g**
- **Protein: 12g**
- **Fat: 2g**
- **Fiber: 11g**
- **Omega 3: 0.3g**
- **Vitamin D: 0 IU**
- **Calcium: 80mg**
- **Iron: 3mg**

DIRECTIONS

1. Layer sweet potato, black beans, tomatoes, bell pepper, and onion in crock pot.
2. Mix in garlic, cumin, chili powder, paprika, salt, and pepper.
3. Pour in vegetable broth.
4. Set crock pot on low, cook for 3 hours.
5. Stir occasionally, serve hot.

ALLERGENS & TIPS

Allergens: Contains legumes (black beans).

Tips: Garnish with fresh cilantro or avocado slices for added flavor. Complements cornbread.

280 KCAL
2 SERVINGS
4 HOURS

VEGETABLE AND LENTIL LOAF

INGREDIENTS

- 1 cup cooked green lentils
- 1 carrot, finely chopped
- 1/2 zucchini, finely chopped
- 1/2 onion, finely diced
- 2 garlic cloves, minced
- 1/4 cup breadcrumbs (30g/1 oz.)
- 1 tbsp olive oil (15ml)
- 1 tsp Italian seasoning
- Salt & pepper to taste
- 1/4 cup tomato sauce (60ml)

DIRECTIONS

1. Sauté onion and garlic in olive oil until translucent.
2. Add carrot and zucchini. Cook until soft.
3. Mix veggies with lentils, breadcrumbs, seasoning, salt, and pepper.
4. Shape into a loaf and place in crock pot.
5. Pour tomato sauce over the top.
6. Cover and cook on low for 4 hours.

NUTRITION

- **Carbs: 48g**
- **Protein: 18g**
- **Fat: 5g**
- **Fiber: 16g**
- **Omega 3: 0.4g**
- **Vitamin D: 0 IU**
- **Calcium: 60mg**
- **Iron: 4mg**

ALLERGENS & TIPS

Allergens: Contains gluten (breadcrumbs).

Tips: Perfect with a side salad or steamed veggies. For extra flavor, add a dash of smoked paprika.

210 KCAL
2 SERVINGS
3 HOURS

STUFFED CABBAGE ROLLS WITH TOMATO SAUCE

INGREDIENTS

- 4 large cabbage leaves
- 1/2 cup brown rice, cooked (90g/3.2 oz.)
- 200g (7 oz.) lean minced turkey
- 1/2 small onion, finely chopped
- 1/4 tsp paprika
- 1 cup tomato sauce (240ml)
- Salt & pepper, as needed
- Fresh parsley for garnish

DIRECTIONS

1. Mix rice, turkey, onion, paprika, salt, and pepper.
2. Boil cabbage leaves for 3 minutes, drain.
3. Place a portion of mixture in each leaf; roll up.
4. Place rolls in crock pot, pour over tomato sauce.
5. Cover, cook on low for 3 hours.
6. Serve hot with fresh parsley.

ALLERGENS & TIPS

Allergens: Contains poultry (turkey). Always ensure tomato sauce is gluten-free if intolerant.

Tips: Fresh tomato sauce is best; if using canned, avoid added sugars. For a richer flavor, sauté onion before mixing. Chopped bell peppers can be added for crunch. Using pre-cooked rice speeds up preparation.

NUTRITION

- **Carbs: 36g**
- **Protein: 22g**
- **Fat: 3g**
- **Fiber: 4g**
- **Omega 3: 0.2g**
- **Vitamin D: 0 IU**
- **Calcium: 70mg**
- **Iron: 2mg**

150KCAL
2 SERVINGS
2 HOURS

LEMON-GARLIC MARINATED OLIVES

INGREDIENTS

- 1 cup green olives (pitted)
- 2 cloves garlic, minced
- Zest of 1 lemon
- 1 tablespoon olive oil
- ½ teaspoon red pepper flakes
- A pinch of salt
- 1/4 cup fresh parsley, chopped

DIRECTIONS

1. In your crock pot, combine olives, garlic, lemon zest, red pepper flakes, and a pinch of salt.
2. Drizzle in the olive oil, giving it a gentle mix to coat everything.
3. Cook on low for 1 hour.
4. Once done, transfer to a bowl and sprinkle with fresh parsley.
5. Allow to marinate for at least an hour before serving.

NUTRITION

- **Carbs: 5g**
- **Protein: 1g**
- **Fat: 15g (healthy fats)**
- **Fiber: 3g**
- **Omega 3: 0.4g**
- **Vitamin D: 0 IU**
- **Calcium: 90mg**
- **Iron: 1.2mg**

ALLERGENS & TIPS

Allergens: Contains olives. Ensure to check for any other allergens depending on the brand or type of olives used.

Advice: Best served chilled. Can be stored in the fridge for up to 3 days for enhanced flavor melding.

CROCK POT POPCORN WITH HERBS

100 KCAL
2 SERVINGS
3 HOURS

INGREDIENTS

- 1/4 cup (60 ml) popcorn kernels
- 1 teaspoon olive oil (it's the good stuff!)
- A sprinkle of sea salt
- 1 teaspoon dried rosemary (or your favorite herb – be creative!)
- 1/2 teaspoon dried thyme

DIRECTIONS

1. Mix those popcorn kernels with the olive oil in the crock pot.
2. Pop the lid on, set to high and let it do its thing. We're talking about 2-3 hours here.
3. Once you hear the pops slowing down, sprinkle in those herbs and salt.
4. Give it a good stir and voila! Herby popcorn goodness!

ALLERGENS & TIPS

Allergens: Popcorn alert! Just in case, some folks might be sensitive.

Quick Tips: Go wild with herbs! Maybe even throw in some nutritional yeast for a cheesy twist without the cheese. Remember, freshness is key! Use recently bought popcorn kernels for the best pop.

NUTRITION

- **Carbs: 15g**
- **Protein: 3g**
- **Fat: 5g (but hey, it's the healthy kind)**
- **Fiber: 4g**
- **Omega 3: 0.2g**
- **Vitamin D: 0 IU**
- **Calcium: 5mg**
- **Iron: 0.5mg**

WARM SPINACH AND ARTICHOKE DIP

150 KCAL
2 SERVINGS
3 HOURS

INGREDIENTS

- 1/2 cup (120 ml) fresh spinach, chopped
- 1/4 cup (60 ml) artichoke hearts, drained and chopped
- 1/4 cup (60 ml) low-fat cream cheese
- 2 tablespoons low-fat Greek yogurt
- 1 garlic clove, minced
- 2 tablespoons grated Parmesan cheese
- A pinch of salt and black pepper

DIRECTIONS

1. In the crock pot, combine spinach, artichokes, cream cheese, Greek yogurt, and garlic.
2. Season with salt and pepper, then stir everything together.
3. Cook on low for 2-3 hours until bubbly and hot.
4. Mix in the Parmesan cheese just before serving

ALLERGENS & TIPS

Allergens: Contains dairy.

Advice: Perfect with carrot sticks or whole-grain crackers. For a little kick, you can add a pinch of red pepper flakes. Enjoy while warm!

NUTRITION

- **Carbs:** 8g
- **Protein:** 9g
- **Fat:** 7g
- **Fiber:** 2g
- **Omega 3:** 0.1g
- **Vitamin D:** 0 IU
- **Calcium:** 160mg
- **Iron:** 1.2mg

ROASTED RED PEPPER HUMMUS

INGREDIENTS

- 1/2 cup (120 ml) canned chickpeas, drained and rinsed
- 1 roasted red pepper (go for jarred to keep it easy!)
- 1 small garlic clove
- 1 tablespoon tahini (sesame paste, if you're wondering!)
- A splash of lemon juice
- 1 tablespoon olive oil (extra virgin, it's the best)
- A dash of cumin, salt, and pepper

DIRECTIONS

1. Chuck those chickpeas, roasted red pepper, garlic, tahini, and lemon juice into the crock pot.
2. Drizzle in that lovely olive oil and sprinkle in your seasonings.
3. Set to low and blend after 3-4 hours until smooth.

NUTRITION

- **Carbs: 20g**
- **Protein: 7g**
- **Fat: 6g**
- **Fiber: 5g**
- **Omega 3: 0.1g**
- **Vitamin D: 0 IU**
- **Calcium: 60mg**
- **Iron: 2.5mg**

ALLERGENS & TIPS

Watch Out: Contains sesame.

Here's a tip: Fancy it up with a sprinkle of paprika on top. And if you're into dipping, veggies or pita bread are A+. Enjoy!

SESAME-GINGER SOY CUCUMBER SALAD

90 KCAL

2 SERVINGS

3 HOURS

INGREDIENTS

- 1 large cucumber, thinly sliced (both metric & imperial, that's about 10 oz or 280g)
- 2 tablespoons soy sauce (30 ml)
- 1 tablespoon sesame oil (15 ml)
- 1 teaspoon grated ginger (5 ml)
- 1 tablespoon white sesame seeds (15 ml)
- A pinch of chili flakes (optional, for a lil' kick!)

DIRECTIONS

1. In your crock pot, combine soy sauce, sesame oil, and grated ginger.
2. Add in the cucumber slices, ensuring they're well-coated with the mix.
3. Let it marinate on low for 2-3 hours.
4. Just before serving, toss in sesame seeds and chili flakes if using.

NUTRITION

- **Carbs: 8g**
- **Protein: 2g**
- **Fat: 5g**
- **Fiber: 1g**
- **Omega 3: 0.2g**
- **Vitamin D: 0 IU**
- **Calcium: 60mg**
- **Iron: 0.7mg**

ALLERGENS & TIPS

Allergens: Contains soy and sesame.

Advice: Best served chilled. Sprinkle some green onions on top for extra freshness and a pop of color! Cheers to tasty salads!

SLOW-COOKED GRANOLA WITH MIXED BERRIES

180 KCAL
2 SERVINGS
2 HOURS

INGREDIENTS

- 1 cup rolled oats (about 90g or 3.2 oz for those into specifics)
- 2 cups mixed berries (yeah, that's roughly 300g or 10.5 oz)
- 2 tablespoons honey (30 ml) – nature's sweet touch!
- 1 teaspoon vanilla extract (5 ml) – trust me, it's the secret ingredient
- 1 cup almond milk (240 ml) – for that creamy texture
- A sprinkle of cinnamon – for some warmth
- 1 tablespoon flaxseeds (15 ml) – for that Omega-3 boost!

DIRECTIONS

1. Mix oats, honey, vanilla extract, cinnamon, and almond milk in your crock pot.
2. Set on low and let it cook for 1.5 hours.
3. Throw in those lovely mixed berries and flaxseeds.
4. Give it another 30 minutes of slow cooking. Voila!

NUTRITION

- **Carbs: 30g**
- **Protein: 5g**
- **Fat: 3g**
- **Fiber: 6g**
- **Omega 3: 1.5g**
- **Vitamin D: 0 IU**
- **Calcium: 150mg**
- **Iron: 1.8mg**

ALLERGENS & TIPS

Allergens: Contains nuts (almonds).

Advice: Top with yogurt for extra creaminess! And remember, this recipe's flexible – swap out berries for your fav fruits. Enjoy!

BALSAMIC GLAZED BRUSSELS SPROUT CHIPS

130 KCAL
2 SERVINGS
2.5 HOURS

INGREDIENTS

- Brussels sprouts, 15 (that's about 200g or 7 oz)
- 2 tablespoons balsamic vinegar (30 ml)
- 1 tablespoon olive oil (15 ml) - but keep it minimal
- A pinch of sea salt
- A whisper of black pepper

DIRECTIONS

1. Clean and peel individual leaves from the Brussels sprouts.
2. Mix balsamic vinegar, olive oil, salt, and pepper in a bowl.
3. Add Brussels sprout leaves, ensuring they're well-coated.
4. Lay them out in the crock pot.
5. Set on low and cook for 2 hours, or until crispy.

NUTRITION

- **Carbs: 14g**
- **Protein: 3g**
- **Fat: 5g**
- **Fiber: 4g**
- **Omega 3: 0.1g**
- **Vitamin D: 0 IU**
- **Calcium: 30mg**
- **Iron: 1mg**

ALLERGENS & TIPS

Allergens: None known. But always double-check if you have specific allergies!

Advice: Best served fresh out the crock pot. Can sprinkle with grated parmesan if desired. Makes for a great side or snack!

VANILLA BEAN RICE PUDDING

185 KCAL
2 SERVINGS
3 HOURS

INGREDIENTS

- ¼ cup (60g) short-grain white rice
- 1 ¾ cups (415ml) skim milk
- 1 vanilla bean, split and seeds scraped
- 1 tablespoon honey
- Pinch of salt
- Ground cinnamon, for garnish (optional)

NUTRITION

- **CARBS: 40g**
- **PROTEIN: 6g**
- **FAT: 0.5g**
- **FIBER: 0.3g**
- **OMEGA 3: 25mg**
- **VITAMIN D: 15 IU**
- **CALCIUM: 150mg**
- **IRON: 0.5mg**

DIRECTIONS

1. Pour milk into the crock pot and warm on low.
2. Toss in the rice and give it a gentle stir.
3. Carefully split your vanilla bean and scrape out those lovely seeds. Toss them into the pot along with the whole bean.
4. Add honey and a pinch of salt.
5. Cover and cook on low for about 3 hours. Check occasionally, giving it a gentle stir.
6. Once the rice is tender and the pudding has thickened, turn off the pot. Remove the vanilla bean.
7. Serve in bowls. Fancy it up with a sprinkle of cinnamon if you like!

ALLERGENS & TIPS

Allergens: Contains dairy (milk).

Tips: Opt for organic vanilla for a deeper flavor. Always check the crock pot's water level.

120 KCAL

2 SERVINGS

1.5 HOURS

MAPLE-GLAZED POACHED FIGS

INGREDIENTS

- 6 fresh figs
- 2 tablespoons maple syrup
- ½ cup (120ml) water
- Zest of half a lemon
- 1 cinnamon stick

DIRECTIONS

1. Place figs at the bottom of the crock pot.
2. Drizzle them lovingly with maple syrup.
3. Pour in water and sprinkle that zest over.
4. Pop the cinnamon stick in for a touch of warmth.
5. Cover and cook on low for 1.5 hours.
6. When soft, carefully transfer figs to serving plates. Drizzle remaining syrup over them.

NUTRITION

- **CARBS: 31g**
- **PROTEIN: 1g**
- **FAT: 0.3g**
- **FIBER: 4g**
- **OMEGA 3: 5mg**
- **VITAMIN D: 0 IU**
- **CALCIUM: 55mg**
- **IRON: 0.6mg**

ALLERGENS & TIPS

Allergens: Contains figs and maple syrup, which can be allergenic for some individuals.

Tips: Top with light yogurt for creaminess. Choose organic maple for genuine sweetness. Rotate figs midway for even syrup distribution.

CINNAMON APPLE CRISP WITH OAT TOPPING

INGREDIENTS

- 2 large apples, peeled and sliced
- 3 tablespoons pure maple syrup
- 1 teaspoon ground cinnamon
- ½ cup (50g) old-fashioned oats
- 1 tablespoon (15g) butter, softened
- A pinch of salt

DIRECTIONS

1. Toss those apple slices in the crock pot.
2. Drizzle them with 2 tablespoons of maple syrup and sprinkle that cinnamon.
3. In a bowl, mix oats, butter, the remaining maple syrup, and salt. Blend until it feels like damp sand.
4. Sprinkle this oat mixture over the apples.
5. Cover, set the pot on low, and let it cook for about 2.5 hours.
6. When those apples are soft and the topping is a bit crispy, it's ready!

ALLERGENS & TIPS

Allergens: Contains oats (gluten) and butter (dairy).

Tips: For a deeper flavor, add a hint of nutmeg. A scoop of low-fat yogurt on top won't hurt either!

NUTRITION

- **CARBS:** 45g
- **PROTEIN:** 3g
- **FAT:** 6g
- **FIBER:** 5g
- **OMEGA 3:** 10mg
- **VITAMIN D:** 0 IU
- **CALCIUM:** 30mg
- **IRON:** 1.2mg

MANGO AND PINEAPPLE SORBET

155 KCAL
2 SERVINGS
3 HOURS

INGREDIENTS

- 1 ripe mango, peeled and diced
- ½ pineapple, peeled and diced
- 2 tablespoons honey or agave nectar
- Juice of half a lime

NUTRITION

- **CARBS: 37g**
- **PROTEIN: 1g**
- **FAT: 0.5g**
- **FIBER: 3g**
- **OMEGA 3: 15mg**
- **VITAMIN D: 0 IU**
- **CALCIUM: 20mg**
- **IRON: 0.4mg**

DIRECTIONS

1. Throw mango and pineapple chunks into the crockpot.
2. Drizzle in the honey or agave, followed by that zesty lime juice.
3. Set the crockpot to low and let it cook for 4 hours. This softens the fruits and melds the flavors.
4. Once done, cool the mixture and then transfer to a blender. Blend until silky smooth.
5. Pour into a container and pop in the freezer until set, typically 3 hours or so.

ALLERGENS & TIPS

Allergens: Contains honey (be wary if allergic).

Tips: Sorbet texture too hard? Blend with a splash of coconut water. Best enjoyed on a sunny day, under some shade.

SLOW-COOKER CHOCOLATE-DIPPED STRAWBERRIES

120 KCAL
2 SERVINGS
2 HOURS

INGREDIENTS

- A dozen strawberries (the fresher, the better, folks!)
- 3 oz (85 grams) dark chocolate (70% cocoa or more - let's keep it heart-healthy!)
- ½ teaspoon coconut oil (just to smoothen things out)

DIRECTIONS

1. Clean those strawberries well and pat 'em dry.
2. In your crockpot, mix the dark chocolate and coconut oil. Set it on low.
3. Wait for an hour or so, until everything's melted and mixed. Stir occasionally.
4. Dip each strawberry into the chocolate, let excess drip off.
5. Place dipped strawberries on parchment paper and let 'em set.

NUTRITION

- **CARBS: 14g**
- **PROTEIN: 1.8g**
- **FAT: 6g (the good kind!)**
- **FIBER: 3g**
- **OMEGA 3: Minimal**
- **VITAMIN D: 0.2µg**
- **CALCIUM: 20mg**
- **IRON: 2mg**

ALLERGENS & TIPS

Allergens: Contains chocolate (which may have traces of milk, nuts, and soy).

Tips: To jazz things up, sprinkle some crushed nuts or desiccated coconut before the chocolate sets.

GINGER AND APRICOT BAKED APPLES

INGREDIENTS

- 2 juicy apples (your favorite kind)
- 4 dried apricots, chopped
- 1 teaspoon fresh ginger, grated
- 1 tablespoon honey
- 1/4 cup water (60 ml)

DIRECTIONS

1. Core those apples but keep the bottom intact.
2. Mix apricots and ginger in a bowl.
3. Spoon that mix into the apples.
4. Drizzle honey over the apples.
5. Pop them in the crockpot, add water.
6. Cook on low for 2 hours or until they're soft but not mushy.

NUTRITION

- **CARBS: 42g**
- **PROTEIN: 0.5g**
- **FAT: 0.3g**
- **FIBER: 5g**
- **OMEGA 3: Minimal**
- **VITAMIN D: 0µg**
- **CALCIUM: 10mg**
- **IRON: 0.2mg**

ALLERGENS & TIPS

Allergens: Contains apricots.

Tips: Try a drizzle of low-fat yogurt on top when serving. Perfecto!

ZUCCHINI CHOCOLATE CAKE

250 KCAL | 2 SERVINGS | 2 HOURS

INGREDIENTS

- 1 cup zucchini, grated (that's about 1 small zucchini)
- 3/4 cup whole wheat flour
- 1/4 cup cocoa powder
- 1/2 teaspoon baking soda
- 1/4 cup coconut sugar (or any other sweetener you fancy)
- 1/4 cup yogurt
- 1 small egg
- A pinch of salt

DIRECTIONS

1. Mix flour, cocoa, baking soda, and salt. That's your dry team!
2. In another bowl, whisk egg, sugar, and yogurt together. The wet squad!
3. Now, add the dry team to the wet squad slowly. Teamwork!
4. Fold in the zucchini. Don't overmix; keep it chill.
5. Pour the batter into a greased crock pot insert.
6. Cover and cook on low for 2 hours. Then, enjoy the magic!

NUTRITION

- **CARBS:** 50g
- **PROTEIN:** 6g
- **FAT:** 4g
- **FIBER:** 3g
- **OMEGA 3:** 0.2g
- **VITAMIN D:** 0.5µg
- **CALCIUM:** 40mg
- **IRON:** 2mg

ALLERGENS & TIPS

Allergens: Contains eggs and dairy.

Tips: For an extra kick, sprinkle some dark choc chips on top. Healthy and delish!

SLOW COOKER CARAMEL FLAN

INGREDIENTS

- 2 large eggs
- ¼ cup skim milk
- 2 tbsp. sugar
- ½ tsp. vanilla extract
- Pinch of salt
- 2 tbsp. water (for caramel)

DIRECTIONS

1. In a saucepan, heat sugar and water until golden-brown. Pour into two ramekins.
2. Whisk eggs, milk, vanilla, and salt. Divide between ramekins.
3. Pour ½ inch water in the crockpot. Place ramekins inside.
4. Cook on low for 3 hours.
5. Let it cool, then refrigerate. Serve upside down

NUTRITION

- **Carbs:** 25g
- **Protein:** 6g
- **Fat:** 8g
- **Fiber:** 0g
- **Omega 3:** 0.1g
- **Vitamin D:** 1.5μg
- **Calcium:** 56mg
- **Iron:** 0.8mg

ALLERGENS & TIPS

Allergens: Contains eggs and dairy.

Tips: Chill for 1 hour for best texture. Loosen flan edges with a knife before flipping. Sprinkle cinnamon for extra flavor punch!

74

Made in the USA
Las Vegas, NV
03 October 2023